My Amazing Toddler Behavioral Series

I Stay Snuggly and Warm.
I'll Feel Better SOON!

An Affirmation-Themed Toddler Book About Being Sick (Ages 2-4)

By Suzanne T. Christian

TWORAVENS
BOOKS

Two Little Ravens
CHILDREN'S NON-FICTION BOOKS

Paperback Edition: 9781964202532
Hardcover Edition: 9781964202549
Digital Edition: 9781964202556

Published in the United States by Two Ravens Books LLC,
254 Chapman Rd, Ste 209, Newark DE 19702

'Expand the mind, free the imagination, one title at a time.'
www.tworavensbooks.com

Welcome to
I Stay Snuggly and Warm. I'll Feel Better Soon!

This book is filled with simple, uplifting affirmations tailored for toddlers ages 2-4. Together, you'll explore comforting routines and gentle encouragement that help little ones cope with sniffles, sneezes, and feeling under the weather

Each page features engaging illustrations and relatable moments, helping children feel brave, loved, and more secure when they're not feeling their best. By making this book a regular part of your reading time, you'll reinforce healthy habits and spark positive self-talk-essential building blocks for emotional well-being.

Prepare for a journey of healing, resilience, and lots of cuddly fun as you and your child discover the power of staying snuggly and warm–even on the toughest sick days!"

Suzanne T. Christian

I cuddle under my warm blanket.
I'll feel better soon!

Achoo,

Achoo,

I blow my nose—
those icky germs
gotta go!

Taking my medicine is yucky,
but it helps me feel better.

A spoonful of soup makes
my tummy warm.
I'll feel better soon!

When I rest, my body fights germs!

I drink water from my special cup—
it's my superhero juice!

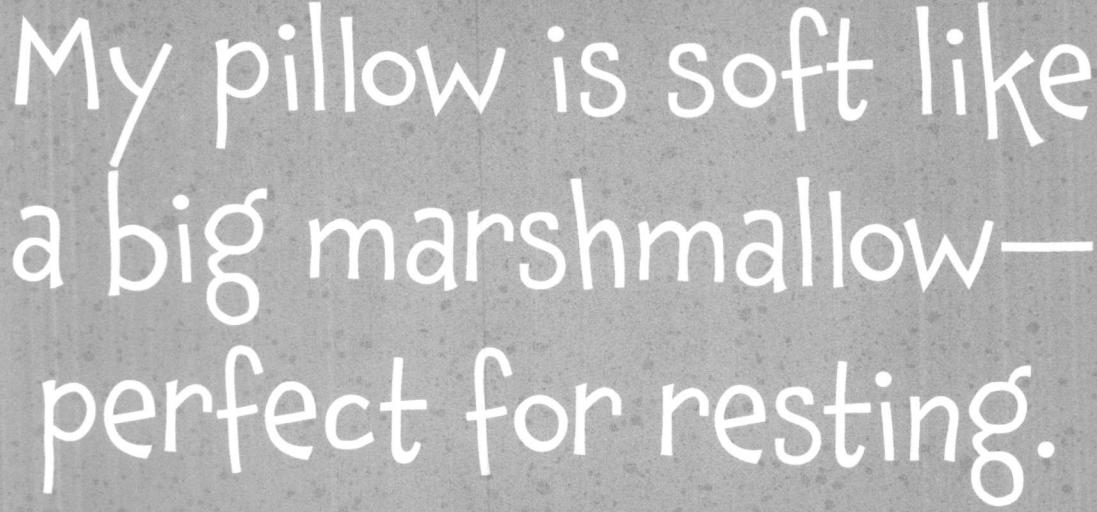

My pillow is soft like a big marshmallow—perfect for resting.

I miss my friends, but they will be so happy when I'm all better!

Cough, cough, sip, sip.
my warm drink helps me feel cozy inside!

I give my teddy bear a pretend check-up—now we both feel brave!

It's okay to feel grumpy when I'm sick.
I'll feel better soon!

I take tiny bites of food to give my belly happy energy!

When I wash my hands,
I say **"Bye-bye!"**
to icky germs.

A cozy nap helps me heal,
so I close my eyes like a sleepy kitten.

cough

cough

Sometimes I cough
like a tiny dragon.
I'll feel better soon!

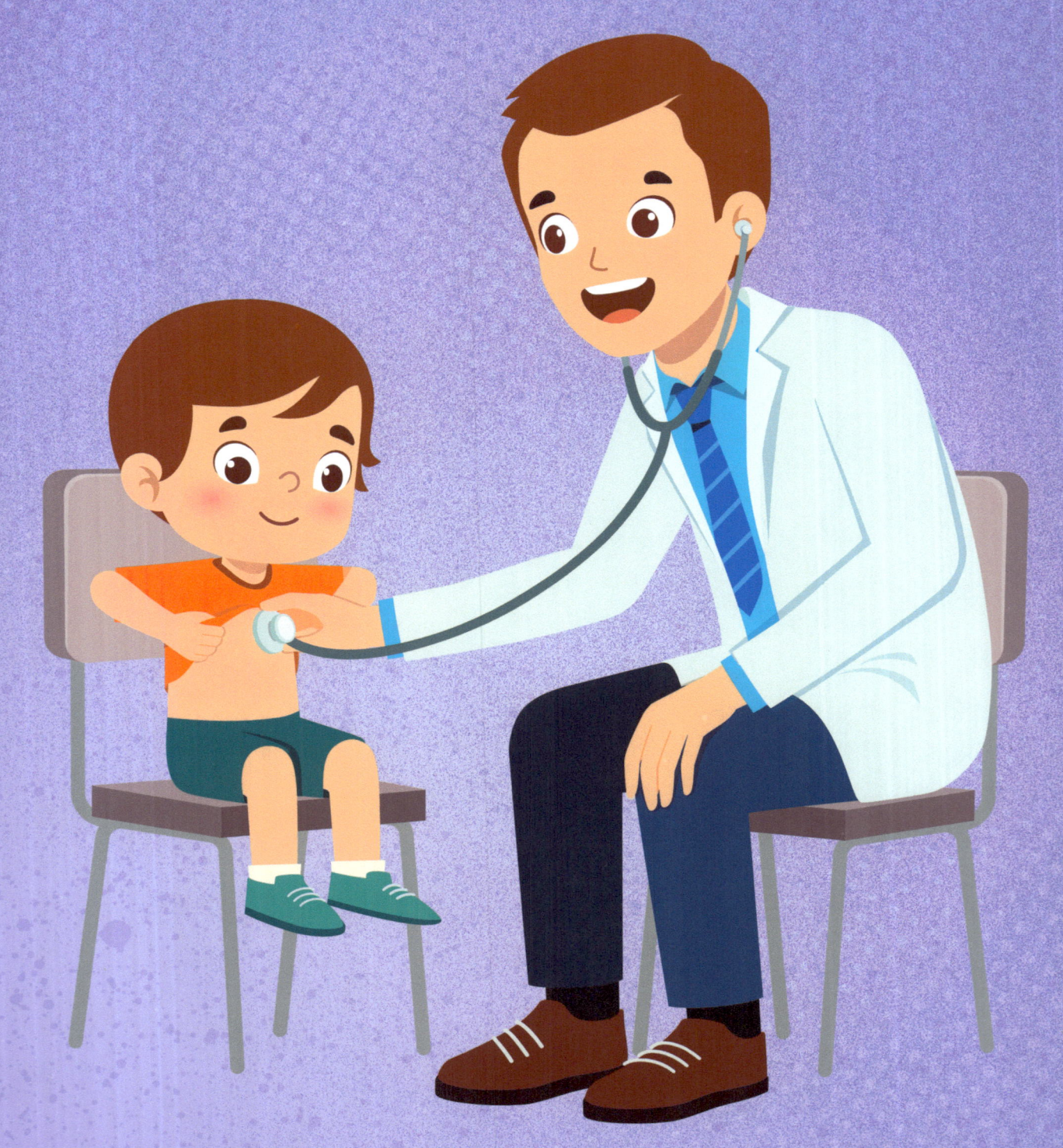

I'm brave when the doctor listens to my chest—no ouchies!

Doctor visits help me get better.

I say, 'Thank you, Doctor!'

Peek-a-boo with my blanket makes me smile, even when I'm sick.

I
Sniffle, Sniffle,
and then use a tissue.

Sniffles don't stop me from being brave.

When I wake up,
I feel a little bit better—
Hooray!

I Stay Snuggly and Warm.

I'll Feel Better SOON!

The End!

My Amazing Toddler Behavioral Series

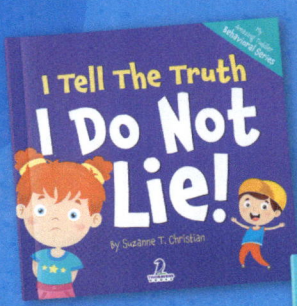

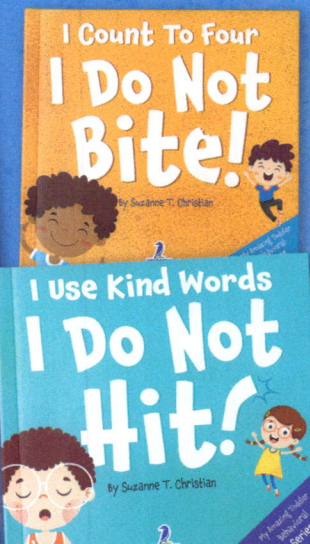

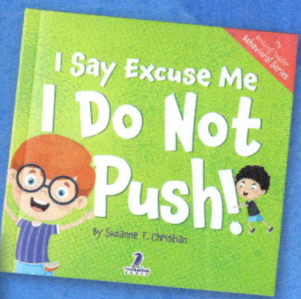

Check Out
Suzanne T. Christian's beloved series
'My Amazing Toddler Behavioral Series'.
Young readers are sure to enjoy!

Dear Amazing Reader,

Thank you for diving into **I Stay Snuggly and Warm. I'll Feel Better Soon!** with me. If this book touched your heart or made a difference for a young reader, I'd be grateful if you could share your thoughts in a review. Your feedback inspires my future work and helps others discover the magic within these pages.

I'd love to hear from you directly if you have suggestions or ideas for improving the book. Please feel free to reach out to me at **suzanne.christian@tworavensbooks.com.** Your voice counts, and I cherish it deeply.

With heartfelt gratitude,